CIVIL RIGHTS LEADERS

MEET MALCOLM X

MELODY S. MIS

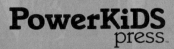

PowerKiDS press

New York

To Donnie Heavener

Published in 2008 by The Rosen Publishing Group, Inc.
29 East 21st Street, New York, NY 10010

First Edition

Editors: Nicole Pristash and Jennifer Way
Book Design: Julio Gil
Photo Researcher: Nicole Pristash

Photo Credits: Cover, back cover, title page, headers, pp. 5, 7, 11, 13, 15, 19 © Getty Images; p. 9 (main, inset) © Time & Life Pictures/Getty Images; pp. 17, 21 © Library of Congress Prints and Photographs Division.

Library of Congress Cataloging-in-Publication Data

Mis, Melody S.
  Meet Malcolm X / Melody S. Mis. — 1st ed.
      p. cm. — (Civil rights leaders)
  Includes index.
  ISBN 978-1-4042-4214-2 (library binding)
  1. X, Malcolm, 1925–1965—Juvenile literature. 2. Black Muslims—Biography—Juvenile literature.
3. African Americans—Biography—Juvenile literature. I. Title.
  BP223.Z8L57637 2008
  320.54'6092—dc22
  [B]
                                                    2007036120

Manufactured in the United States of America

Contents

Meet Malcolm X

In 1965, Malcolm X gave a speech that shocked America. He said that African Americans should use "any means necessary" to get freedom. This suggested that blacks should use **violent** actions to gain equality.

Malcolm's ideas were different from those of other leaders of the **civil rights movement**. He went against Martin Luther King Jr.'s idea of using peaceful **protests** to gain equality. Malcolm's belief that blacks could improve their life by using violence angered a lot of people. Many agreed, though, and Malcolm became one of the greatest civil rights leaders of all time.

The civil rights movement is the name given to African Americans' struggle for equal rights. It began with Martin Luther King Jr.'s protest marches of the 1960s.

Malcolm X did not want people to hurt each other for no reason. However, he believed that violence was sometimes necessary to fight inequality.

Malcolm Little was born on May 19, 1925, in Omaha, Nebraska. When Malcolm was young, his father often spoke out against **segregation**. This angered members of the Black Legion, who set fire to the Littles' house in 1929.

When Malcolm was six, his father died. Then, his mother got sick and Malcolm had to go live with another family. Despite his troubled home life, Malcolm made good grades in school. He even wanted to be a **lawyer**. A teacher, however, told Malcolm he should not try to be a lawyer because he was black. After that, Malcolm lost interest in school and quit at age 15.

The Black Legion was a group whose members believed white people were better than people of other races. The Black Legion was known for using violence to scare or harm African Americans.

The Ku Klux Klan (KKK), shown here, is a group of whites that is against blacks. In 1924, the KKK wanted to hurt Malcolm's father because he was against segregation.

In 1940, Malcolm moved to Boston, Massachusetts, where he lived with his sister. He took a job shining shoes at a dance hall. Malcolm was doing well but he started getting into trouble with his friends. Soon, he began selling illegal drugs.

Malcolm moved to New York City in 1943, where he continued a life of crime. Malcolm robbed people and **gambled** illegally. He made a lot of money by selling drugs, robbing, and doing bad things to people. His days of crime would be over soon, though. Malcolm moved back to Boston in 1946. He was caught there and was sent to prison for six years.

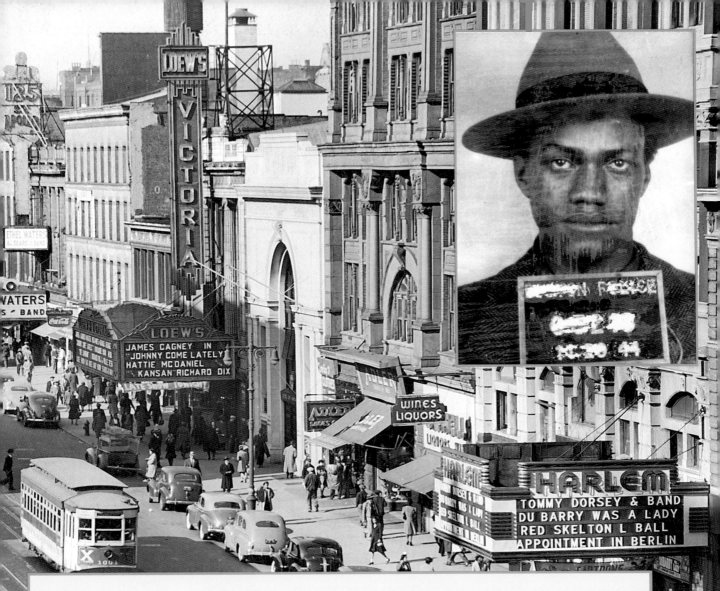

While in New York City, Malcolm X lived in a neighborhood called Harlem, shown here. *Inset:* This picture was taken when Malcolm X was arrested in 1944.

Malcolm hated prison. One day, he met a prisoner named Bimbi. This meeting changed Malcolm's life. Bimbi **encouraged** Malcolm to educate, or teach, himself by reading books from the prison library. Malcolm listened. He even took classes by mail.

Malcolm's brother, Reginald, told him about a new **organization** called the Nation of Islam, or NOI. The NOI is a group that practices a form of the **religion** called Islam. Reginald thought this religion might help Malcolm. While in prison, Malcolm joined the NOI.

Islam is a religion founded in the seventh century by Muhammad, a religious figure. People who believe in Islam are called Muslims. They follow laws that are set down in a book called the Koran.

Elijah Muhammad, shown here, was the leader of the Nation of Islam during Malcolm X's lifetime. Muhammad became Malcolm's mentor, or teacher.

The NOI is a black religious organization. Its members are called Black Muslims. The NOI is different from Islam because its purpose is to make life better for blacks. The NOI used to believe that blacks should be kept away from whites. It even wanted blacks to have their own nation because it believed all white people were bad.

When Malcolm joined the NOI, he changed his last name to X. He was a very powerful speaker and he soon became a leader. Newspaper and television reporters followed Malcolm to hear his ideas and his speeches on **racism**.

X stands for an African American's real name, which was lost when he became a slave. A slave was usually given the last name of the person who owned him.

As leader of the NOI, Malcolm X made many speeches across America. Here he is giving a speech in Washington, D.C., in 1962.

A Trip to Mecca

In 1964, Malcolm X went to visit Mecca, Islam's most important place, in the Middle East. There, he saw Muslims of all races being friendly to each other. He learned that true Muslims believe all races are equal. This changed Malcolm's mind about the NOI's teachings. He no longer believed that all whites were bad. Malcolm still thought, however, that whites in America had too much power over blacks.

After Malcolm left Mecca, he visited other African countries. He realized that Africans had suffered through the same struggle. Malcolm decided that blacks all over the world should join together to fight racism.

Islam requires that all Muslims visit Mecca, shown here, at least once during their lifetime. Around 3 million people visit Mecca every year!

The OAAU

Before going to Africa, Malcolm X had a disagreement with the leaders of the NOI. He no longer believed they were doing their best to help blacks get equal rights. After his return, Malcolm left the NOI. He formed the Organization of Afro-American Unity (OAAU).

The OAAU's chief purpose was for all blacks to be able to take care of themselves, without white people's help. It wanted blacks to control their own life. The OAAU **promoted** black pride, schooling, and the importance of voting. It encouraged blacks to keep themselves safe from racist people, even if it meant using violence.

On February 14, 1965, Malcolm's home was set on fire. No one was hurt. Many people believe that the NOI burned it because Malcolm had left the organization.

Malcolm X's ideas about violence scared many people. Malcolm wanted people to better understand him and his ideas. He therefore worked on a book about his life with a black author named Alex Haley. It is called *The Autobiography of Malcolm X.*

Malcolm's book presents the problems blacks have suffered under a government controlled by whites. It also tells how Malcolm X rose up from poor beginnings to become a respected leader. Malcolm's book tells African Americans they should be proud of being black. It also tells them never to stop fighting for equality and rights.

Alex Haley, shown here, wrote *The Autobiography of Malcolm X* based on meetings with Malcolm. His book became a very important African-American work.

Unafraid

Malcolm X knew he might be killed because of his actions and his strong beliefs. Before he left the Nation of Islam in 1964, several members had wanted him dead. Malcolm had become too powerful and too famous. The NOI did not like that. Malcolm knew his life was in danger, but he continued to speak out.

On February 21, 1965, Malcolm had just begun to speak at an OAAU meeting when shots were fired. Malcolm X was shot dead. Many believe the men who killed him were members of the NOI. They were sent to prison for their crime.

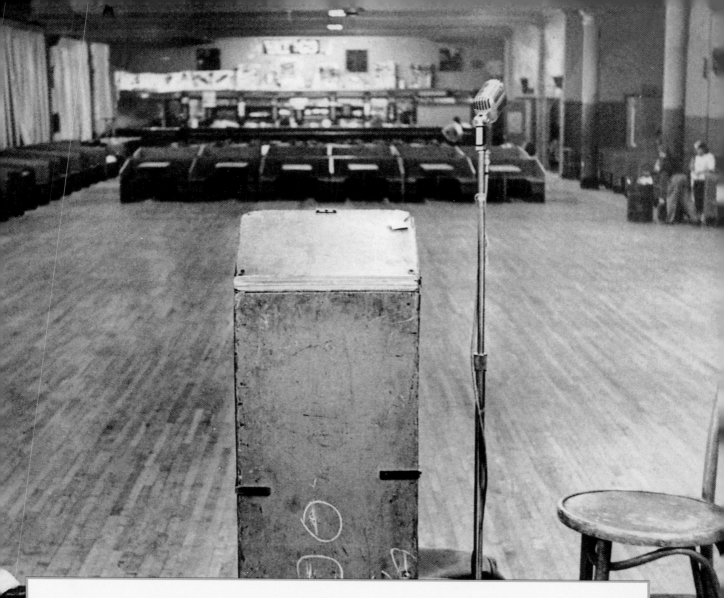

This is the hall in which Malcolm X was killed. It is located at the Audubon Ballroom in Harlem, New York City.

Malcolm X was one of the most powerful leaders of the civil rights movement. He often used violent words and encouraged violent actions. That was his way of getting people to listen. Once people listened, they could better understand the problems blacks faced.

In the end, Malcolm wanted black freedom. He believed blacks could gain freedom if they fought for it. Malcolm encouraged blacks to take control of their own life. Malcolm taught blacks to respect themselves and their history. For that reason, he is known as a **symbol** of black pride.

civil rights movement (SIH-vul RYTS MOOV-mint) People and groups working together to win freedom and equality for all.

encouraged (in-KUR-ijd) Gave someone reason to do something.

gambled (GAM-buld) Bet money on the result of something.

lawyer (LAH-yer) A person who acts for others in court.

organization (or-guh-nih-ZAY-shun) A group of people who meet for a purpose.

promoted (pruh-MOHT-ed) Raised attention about something.

protests (PROH-tests) Acts of disagreement.

racism (RAY-sih-zum) The belief that one group or race is better than another.

religion (rih-LIH-jen) A way of honoring a god or gods.

segregation (seh-grih-GAY-shun) The act of keeping one group of people away from another group of people.

symbol (SIM-bul) A person or object that stands for something important.

violent (VY-lent) Having or showing great force.

Index

Web Sites

Due to the changing nature of Internet links, PowerKids Press has developed an online list of Web sites related to the subject of this book. This site is updated regularly. Please use this link to access the list:
www.powerkidslinks.com/crl/malx/